CHRIST
and a
Chinese Family

Gilbert C. Nee

To

Asbury College Library

from
the author

Gilbert Ree

GILBERT C. NEE

CHRIST
AND A
CHINESE FAMILY

By

G. C. Nee, A. B.

AUTHOR OF

"The New Birth," in Chinese; "The Man That Is
Born From Above," to be published in Chinese;
the editor of "The Voices of Many
Lands," in English

INTRODUCTION BY
Z. T. JOHNSON, Ph. D.
Vice President, Asbury College

FOREWORD BY
FRANK P. MORRIS, D. D.
Professor Systematic Theology, Asbury Theological
Seminary

"JESUS ONLY"

To My Mother
MRS. DORCAS NEE
To whom
I owe my life and Christian faith
This book is most affectionately
dedicated

INTRODUCTION

I have read the manuscript by Mr. Gilbert C. Nee entitled, *Christ and a Chinese Family*. Having become acquainted with Mr. Nee as a senior in Asbury College during the current year, I have been greatly pleased with his attitude as a student, a Christian, and a willing worker in attempting to earn his way through college.

From the viewpoint of historical philosophy, I think the chapter on "Religions and the Chinese People" warrants the publication of this book. It gives a comparative statement of the religions of the Chinese people. It is interesting also to note that although historians deny that Confucianism is a religion, Mr. Nee shows from his own personal relationships that it is, at least in the mind of the average Chinese person, a "system of religious and ethical teachings, which is the essential source of Chinese civilization."

From the viewpoint of religious experience, the chapter on "Christ and My Mother" is exceedingly interesting. This, with the chapter on "Christ and I," gives an intimate picture of the religious strivings in a typical Chinese home. It is certainly worth reading.

It gives me pleasure to commend not only this book, but also the author, to the cordial support of Christian friends.

Z. T. JOHNSON,
Vice-President Asbury College.

FOREWORD

For almost two years I have known Mr. G. C. Nee, the author of this well-written volume. It has been the pleasure and intimacy of teacher and student, ripening into a precious friendship and fellowship of those of like faith. It was with real pleasure I have just read the book, "Christ and a Chinese Family," written by Mr. Nee. My love and admiration for him added a peculiar note of interest. But as I read on, I soon found I was really being instructed in the great religions of China, and her habits and customs, and the richness of the Chinese character; and with it all the great hunger of heart for that life that is found only in Christ. This he has beautifully and vividly illustrated in the story of the power of Christ as wrought out in his own family, including himself and his mother.

Then his final careful appraisal of China as an open field of opportunity is well worthy of most careful consideration. I want to thank Mr. Nee for his book. He has sounded a note of faith and courage and devotion, and withal, of intelligence which we all need, and which merits careful study. The Lord add his blessing to author and reader abundantly.

Heartily,

FRANK P. MORRIS

Professor Systematic Theology, Asbury Theological Seminary, Wilmore, Ky.

AUTHOR'S PREFACE

In June, 1934, while I was in London, one day, I was in the British Chief Passport Office, British Passport Control, talking with a young Jewish gentleman who studied law in the University of London and was getting his passport to return home to Palestine. I told him about my Christian experience with the purpose of winning this young Jew to become a Christian. This thoughtful young man frankly challenged me to give him some adequate reasons why I abandoned my original native faith and accepted Christianity. Quick as a flash I asked the Lord in my heart to help me; then I immediately answered him and gave him four reasons as to why I accepted Christianity and why I believe that Jesus is the Messiah. In return I proceeded to challenge him to accept Jesus as his personal Savior and Christ. His eyes were wet as he promised me to read the New Testament. The time came when we had to shake hands and say "Goodbye" to each other. He left for Palestine, and I got my Vise and left for Norway and other countries beyond.

From the time of this experience I have believed that a man who rejects all other religions and accepts Christianity ought to be able to give a reason for it. (1 Peter 3:15)

There are many forms of religion on the earth, but there must be one true religion; for there is only one true God in the universe, so there can be only one true revelation. Christianity proves to be the one!

Therefore it is the purpose of this booklet to present a short story of the author's home and life giving his reasons to the world for his conversion from the heathen religions—Taoism, Buddhism, and Confucianism — to Christianity, the true, absolute religion.

The author hopes that this little book will reach some of his Jewish brothers. It is also the writer's hope that this booklet may set forth the glory of

God in His saving grace which reaches out to all humanity alike, and that it may also testify to the fact that the true Mission is worthwhile and necessary.

My thanks are given to Professor Marie Sprague who kindly undertook to read and correct the proof. I am also grateful to Dr. Z. T. Johnson, Dr. F. H. Larabee, Dr. F. P. Morris, and Professor W. D. Turkington who read the manuscript and gave their kind remarks.

GILBERT CHIBEE NEE.

Wilmore, Kentucky.
January, 1, 1936.

CONTENTS.

CHAPTER I.

RELIGIONS AND THE CHINESE PEOPLE

THE RELIGIOUS NATURE OF MAN

One of the fixed elements of human psychology is that human beings are incurably religious! Men will worship, and they want to worship; for the human soul cannot always look down or around, it must also look up. Man is the "upward-looking animal" and "a moral-beaten creature." This is his highest faculty and distinction.

We are made with a religious and moral nature and sense, endowed with the capacities of God's infiniteness that draws us Godward and keeps us lingering on the divine side.

The religious instinct is universal, so religion becomes the universal fact. As far back as history and archæology are able to penetrate the dim beginning of human life, man had a religion. It is found among all nations. However ruined, alienated, degraded they may be there existed in all a universal instinct seeking its satisfaction and manifesting itself in religious forms and ceremonies.

Plutarch says, "You may see states without walls, without laws, without coins, without writings, but a people without a god, or without religious exercise and sacrifices, has no man seen. For a consciousness of the existence of God everywhere exists, and man cannot think of God without attributing to himself some kind of relation toward Him."

His religious nature will immediately impel him to live a religious life, just as he has a physical and a social nature which impels him to live a physical and social life. Human nature is universally the same anywhere under the sun.

As man lived in the sunlighted world and enjoyed sunshine, moon, stars, and nature before they studied astronomy and physics, and had desire for food long before they knew anything about dietetics and chemistry, so they worshipped God before they so much as thought about theology or theosophy! The religious nature is just as constitutional and ineradicable in man as the mental or physical; therefore, he is necessarily and incurably religious!

A man's religion is the expression of the whole fabric of his inner being and a natural attitude in relation to which he adjusts himself to the universe and the world of nature round about him. It is a desire to fulfill this spiritual need and to restore his original relation of mastership and friendship with God, his Creator and Father.

Religion, moreover, deals most powerfully and directly with our moral, intellectual, and social realm of life. From the primitive time down to the present century religion has played its part at every stage in the course of human development. Of course, the forms of religion vary with the condition of our standard of knowledge and thinking. The form of man's development depends on the type of religion he entertains, and vice versa.

THE RELIGIOUS LIFE OF CHINESE PEOPLE

What was the earliest type of Chinese religion? What was the original religion of the Chinese? These questions have been a subject of much controversy.

In a study of our Chinese character, the words, "Shang-ti," for the Supreme Being, would indicate that the idea back of it was monotheistic, and undoubtedly there has been the conception among the Chinese of worshipping a Supreme Being—God—raised high above all other gods which was later mixed up with their religious thinking and worship, just like the Hebrews at first believed in one God, but later when they came into Canaan the people mixed with the polytheism of heathen religion and became idolatrous.

CHINESE RELIGIONS AND GODS

There are three religions in China; not Mohammedanism which has always been taken as strange and foreign, but Taoism, Confucianism and Buddhism. These three religions have been dominating Chinese religious thinking and nature, shaping lives, customs, and cultures as they have been and as they are going to be. Underneath all these religions and the multitudinous forms of religious ceremonies are the Chinese religious attitudes and life which have existed for centuries and centuries.

TAOISM

The founder of the mystical Taoism was Loa-Tze who is supposed to have been born in 604 B. C. Taoism is the native religion and exists only in China, standing in contrast with Confucianism and Buddhism.

"Tao" is somewhat equivalent to Logos, Word, or Way; its actual meaning is referred to "The Principle of Nature," "The Essence of the Uni-

verse," or "The Cosmic Process."   It is
the explanation of the universe and im-
mortality.   Tao speaks about the creation, nature, virtue, ethics, Hades, and
heaven.   The ideas are very much different from those of Christianity.

Taoism is a rather primitive form of
religion, and it is animistic in nature
and character.   It is a belief in spirits
inhabiting all natural objects, animate
and inanimate, good and bad, strong
and weak.   They are to be found everywhere, on the mountains, among the
trees, in the ground, and under the water.   Everything that happens is ac-
counted for by spiritual agencies. Sick-
ness is caused by demons within the
body which must be exorcised.   In ac-
cord with this a child is drowned not by
any natural cause, but because a fiend-
ish spirit catches him from under the
water and draws him down. These
spirits, invisible as they flit about
through the air, are exceedingly real.
There are innumerable superstitions in

Taoism.

Taoism thus embraces all of China's countless primitive beliefs to its bosom and becomes a conglomeration of superstitions. The dread of spirits and demons is the nightmare of Chinese life. Here is the ministration of demons instead of angels!

Taoism exercises exorcists and witches and other similar devilish methods for deliverance from human sufferings and calamities. There are Taoist temples built everywhere; idols are worshipped; shrines are found in all places, on hills, on roadsides, and in every home. Hundreds of Taoist priests are hired annually by the villagers; ceremonies are strictly observed, and big sums of money are sometimes spent for the purpose. During certain festivals, especially during the Chinese New Year Day, the idols are carried with a big parade through the villages in order to please the gods. An average Chinese person serves more than one god.

It is interesting to note that Chinese people accept Taoism, believe its doctrine, and worship the spirits of its noble followers, but never worship its founder, Loa-Tze.

Laying aside the idolatry and the adoration of the creature more than the great Creator, it is a mixture of spirit worship, superstition, charms, witchcraft, and demonology. It is degrading to the intellect and a degenerating force among the Chinese people. There is little hope for China, politically, religiously, morally, or economically until Taoism is swept from the face of the land!

CONFUCIANISM

Confucius lived from B. C. 551-478. He appeared in China as a great political and ethical teacher and a reformer of the social condition of that day, five centuries before the Christian era. Confucianism, unlike Taoism, is that system of religious and ethical teaching which is the essential source of Chinese civilization.

Confucius' contributions to the literary world of China are: Five-king, or Five Canonical Volumes, such as the *Book of Ancient History*, the *Book of Ancient Poems*, the *Book of Ancient Rites and Ceremonies*, the *Book of Changes*, and of *Spring and Autumn;* and Four Shoo, or his Writings, such as *Analects, Great Learnings, Doctrine of Mean*, and *The Work of Mecius.*

For two thousand years or more these sacred volumes have been the substratum of Chinese literature. They are the principal textbooks in all institutions of learning. There is no possibility of political preferment without being thoroughly familiar with the Five King and the Four Shoo. Chinese people take them as their Bible. The literati are the ruling class. There is no promotion except for scholarship. Once in three years there is an examination of candidates for degrees. No student can be entered as a candidate unless he has previously studied the whole system of Confucius. The successful competitors, in the course of time, become the rulers of the empire. Thus it is evident that China, commonly regarded as a monarchy, is really an aristocracy, an aristocracy of learning.

The aim of Confucius was to reform the corrupted government of China of that day, a reform which he believed ought to be accomplished by the reviving of certain healthy principles which had prevailed in the traditional Golden Age. The learning of his time consisted of the study of the literature that had come down from the earlier ages. He claimed to be the student of Antiquity. In his learning Confucius first became a devoted pupil and later a distinguished Master of the ages.

Confucius' teachings emphasize man's duty toward men rather than man's duty toward God. His teaching recognizes five sets of social relationships; those between rulers and subjects, father and son, husband and wife, elder brothers and younger brothers, friends and friends. Reverence and obedience are always due to the superiors. Three-fifths of the human relations are concerned with the family which is the vital factor of Chinese life. Filial piety is absolutely required in the family and is considered the highest virtue among morals. Social customs, too, lay great stress on the family relation. Filial piety has been influential to a large degree in the preservation of the family, and the family in turn, has held the nation together for centuries, in spite of internal disturbance and foreign encroachment.

Confucius explained: "What is meant by 'In order rightly to govern the state, it is necessary first to regulate the family.' It is not possible for one to teach others, while he cannot teach his own family. Therefore the ruler, without going beyond his family, completes the lessons for the state. There is filial piety; therewith the sovereign should be served. There is fraternal submission; therewith elders and superiors should be served. There is kindness: therewith the multitude (the friendship relation) should be treated."

Confucius' social order:

"Wishing to order their own state, they first regulate their own family; wishing to regulate their own family, they cultivate their own person; wishing to cultivate their own person, they first rectify their heart; wishing to rectify their heart, they first ought to be sincere in their thought; wishing to be sincere in their thought, they first extend to the utmost their knowledge. Such extension of their knowledge lay in the investigation of the things. Things being investigated, knowledge becomes complete. Their knowledge becoming complete, thought becomes sincere; their thought being sincere, their hearts were then rectified; their hearts being rectified, their persons were cultivated; their persons being cultivated, their families were regulated; their families being regulated, their states were rightly governed; their states being rightly governed, the whole kingdom was made tranquil and happy. From the Son of Heaven (the Emperor) down to the masses of people all must consider the cultivation of the persons, the root of everything besides.

"From the loving example of one family a whole State becomes loving, and from its courtesies the whole State becomes courteous, while from the ambition and perverseness of the one man, the whole State may be led to rebellious disorder, such is the nature of influence. This may be verified by the saying 'Affairs may be ruined by a single sentence, a kingdom may be settled by its one man.' "

There is recorded how the noble human Confucius anticipated the Golden Rule of Christianity which was to be pronounced by Christ centuries later. Tsu-Kung had asked him, "Is there any one word which may serve as a rule of practice for daily life?"   Confucius turned his serene face upon him and answered, "What you would not have done to yourself do not to others." Confucius built his golden rule in a negative way compared with Christ's, "As you would that men should do to you, do you also to them likewise."

Confucius knew little about gods, cared less, and discouraged prayer. "So long as you do not know how to serve men, how can you serve the spirits?" Once when asked about future life and death he said, "So long as you do not know life how can you know death?" Wisdom consists in serving other men and in respecting the spirits without making a fuss over them. He knew that what a superior man sought was to be found only within himself.

Peace and safety and prosperity are substantial blessings to be sought for and enjoyed. So the Chinese people have a proverb which runs in this wise:

"The Buddhist priests declare Fo in the
    abyss to be;
Say Taoist's followers, Paradise lies
    in the Southern Sea;
But great Confucius' pupils look on
    real things around,
Before their eyes the air of spring,
    fresh blowing, brush the ground."

Confucianism can hardly be classified as a religion, but rather as an ethical system.   The interest of Confucianism is ethical and social rather than religious.   The world today calls it a religion because Chinese people wanted it
to be a religion and worship it.   For at
least 1,200 years, twice each year, in
the temple of Confucius at the old capi-
tal of Pieping, the emperor of China
has conducted religious worship of Confucius, with a ritual of praise and sacrificial offerings.

On earth he had for years no home;
he now has 1,500 temples throughout
the cities of China.   Many times he
starved when he was on earth; now he

has over 62,000 animals slaughtered on the altars for offerings to him. He saw no use of prayer; now millions of prayers are lifted to him daily. On earth he did not care for any gods; he has now become a god himself.

However, in recent years the temples of Confucius have been notoriously neglected.

Confucius gave China the intellectual desire and the moral code, but he left the Chinese spiritual craving untouched. His teaching has molded Chinese thinking and bent the mind around his ideas. Chinese people have so long been reading the dull and unattractive maxims of the sages that their minds are benumbed. They are doing as Confucius bade them, walking in the old path again and again. The people are brought up with an absolute absence of independent and creative thinking. The whole policy of state and people is repressive and at a standstill, backward in thinking, and without any creative, forward movement. It halts the Century of Progress of China, and it keeps the nation behind in the race of the modern civilization of the world. In order to nurture Chinese youth for a creative thinking the old Confucius' system of education must completely give way!

BUDDHISM

Buddhism, unlike Taoism and Confucianism, started in India and went northward to Tibet, southward to Ceylon, eastward to Burma and Annan, and from thence conquered China and Japan. Thus the history of eastern Asia is largely the history of Buddhism. It is the principal religion of one-half of Asia. For more than twenty centuries it has swayed the destiny and bent the minds of uncounted millions of men.

Buddhism began in China about 64 A. D. From thence it influenced Korea and Japan like Confucianism.

China is Confucianist, Taoist, and

now also Buddhist. When Buddhism came to China it offered a personal god and idolized Buddha whose calm face and round-bellied body might be seen, kissed, and kow-towed to in every temple. Moreover, it told much of life after death on which Confucianism was silent. Buddhism had its Californian heavens and its Sahara hells—thousands of them—and made prayer for the dead an imperative necessity. Most of all, it was a religion of salvation; belief in Buddha would make life's murk as bright as day. It was what it promised to the Chinese people. Today the Buddhist temples and pagodas are seen all over the country distinguishing it from the Christian countries where we can see crosses everywhere!

Buddhism is a pessimistic philosophy of religion. In all, its effort is to solve the problem of human existence and to devise a way of deliverance from the physical ills and moral evils by asceticism and cutting off all the desires of life. Existence is an unreality due to ignorance and illusion. Life is a great illusion; life is suffering and sorrow. The only salvation or escape is that made into the unconscious calm of Annihilism—Nirvana which is the Buddhist heaven.

In Buddhism the body is regarded with loathing as a mass of corruption, the abode of all evils in the prison-house of man. An aescetic life with its complete separation from the world is the only path for a sure advance in that virtue which assures Nirvana.

Salvation means an escape from existence. There is no place for forgiveness of sin, for there is no God of infinite love and power like Christ the Savior to redeem from the power of sin and death and to make possible a life of everlasting harmony with God.

Salvation is the self-wrought thing striving after Nirvana, abandoning home if necessary, entering a solitary life and pursuing only right action, keeping "The Precepts," and suppressing desires. The intellect must conquer the heart; feeling must give way to meditation. The sense must be dulled. Nirvana is gained by the victory of sublime indifference to everything in life.

Many lives find it impossible to obtain salvation; they are doomed for the hells which have a partial and temporary part in the punishment. The soul reaps what he has sown in his life; the successive Rebirth for ages is necessary to complete the expiration; according to the eternal cycle runs the law of the "Karma."

The difference between Christianity and Buddhism is that in Christianity God Himself saves lost humanity through Christ. The Christian gospel teaches us to prize the gift of personal life as the most sacred and the most precious of all things; for these bodies of ours are the temples of the Holy Spirit of God. We rejoice in tribula-

The Idols in the Buddhist temple and the Dragon—
the ancient Chinese national emblem

tion and suffering, for we know that by His grace through temporal fiery suffering will come out the beauty and glistening gold of life.

Buddhism has a high system of morality; it sets up a high ideal of life; and it teaches the deepest philosophy of the Orient, yet frankly and truly it disappoints many earnest souls and utterly disgraces the human race and extinguishes personal existence.

THE COMPROMISE OF THE CHINESE RELIGIONS

These three religions are very much mixed up with each other on account of the religious demand of the people. Every Chinese home belongs to two or three of these religions; an average person has more than one god for his own. Only Christianity in China is an exclusive and non-compromising religion. Therefore it stands distinct and yet influential.

The Chinese speak of Confucianism,

Buddhism, and Taoism as three religions of the Middle Kingdom. Though the Confucianists belong exclusively to the literary class they worship in Buddhist temples and use the Taoist rituals. The priests of Buddhism and Taoism are the only real Buddhists and Taoists, yet the people hire them in either Buddhist or Taoist ceremonial services, as the people do not consider that they themselves belong to either of these faiths. They regularly burn incense at their temples or shrines and contribute systematically to their support.

The multitude of people, while professing to be Confucianists, do not hesitate to patronize at the same time the temples or shrines of Buddhism and Taoism. Therefore, though this great Master taught them to worship nothing, the empire swarms with millions of gods.

Chinese people are busy with religious duties in various temples; they pay their homage and tribute to the different faiths at various times of the year. They burn incense to Taoist gods today, and they worship in Buddhist temples the next day. At the same time they read Confucius' books, professing to be his disciples!

China is one of the few countries in the world where these three distinctive faiths could stand side by side without collision, and for centuries the Chinese people have been observing the rites of these various faiths.

THE ESSENCE IS GOD AND CHRIST

These various faiths exist in China only because they meet the felt need and answer to the moods of the Chinese soul and the religious requirements.

Confucianism makes plain their duties; Taoism ministers to their superstitious fear; and Buddhism opens up a spiritual world to give them promise of future blessedness.

Chinese people have gone through

their religious struggles seeking for something that is lasting and real for their hungry souls, but, alas, they have not found yet that which will meet their deepest need!

For centuries Chinese have been astray on a way in which they hoped to find a truer God. The masses of people are brought into a cloud of mysticism of faiths not knowing where they are going.

Confucius offered to say something about God, but his idea was vague and obscure. He used "Heaven" as symbolizing God. He made no contribution whatever to the people on the conception of God.

Buddhism is completely silent on this important matter, for Buddhism does not believe in God, except the Buddha.

Taoism tried to meet the need by appointing a human being for a god. As a matter of history in the Sung Dynasty, about a thousand years ago, the Emperor conferred upon a magician and monk of the Han Dynasty by the name of Chang Yi, the title of "Shang Ti," the Jade Emperor or Pearly Emperor, the Supreme Ruler of the Universe. What a claim for the man-made Emperor of the Heaven! He is the king of gods and the ruler of the universe. Chinese people blindly found the concept of one deity and accepted him as their Optimus Maximus and thus hail him as God!

Moreover there is a solitary place in China where homage is paid to the Deity. Near by the city of Peiping is a temple over which in the gateway is inscribed, "To The Supreme Ruler of the Universe." On the first and fifteenth day of each month every Chinese home burns incense in the front of the courtyard to the God of Heaven. Once every year, with magnificent parade, the Emperor of China comes alone as the representative of the nation to offer sacrifice—a bullock—on the Altar of The Heaven in Peiping. Chinese people believe there is a true God behind the universe, but do not know who and what He is or how to find Him and worship Him!

With all the paganism and the heathen ideas of God, as above stated, with the whole measure of their truth there is contained some dim outlines of a holy and true God who created the universe. There is something further in these systems of religions which we cannot overlook, that is, the essence of their religious desire is Christ! It is dim, indeed, but their one desire is for One who shall somehow deliver the world from the consequences of sin and help it to regain the paradise! I rejoice to know that even the nations that lie in darkness and shadow of death are not godless or Christless. They have slender clues of gospel truth, which, were they followed, would lead bewildered souls out of the darkness into the daylight.

Human beings are from God, and are somehow lost, but they want to come back to God. Man is made in such a way that he will never rest until he finds rest in God.

Dr. James H. Snowden declares, "All human life thus points beyond itself for its completion and satisfaction. The human soul swarms with instincts, needs, feeling, thoughts, visions, and aspirations which look beyond the present world and cry out for the Infinite and Eternal. Life that stops at the horizon of this world and the edge of the grave is a poor and pitiful fragment, a hopeless failure, and cruel disappointment. Instinct, feeling, and thought will feel after and fix their filaments on God and cling to him so tight they refuse to be torn loose. The whole human soul is one great cry for God that has filled all the ages, and it will never be stilled and satisfied until it receives His fulness."

Taoism:

There is very little of evil in the world. No human being is to be held responsible. A man may be a fool and a sufferer, but he is not a sinner. Religion is exercised in humbly following the serene divine. "Way" (Tao) the "return to the Nature"—becoming gods.

Confucianism:

The man is born for uprightness. The tendency of man's nature is good. The fundamental evil is social impropriety. A social program of salvation is to be obtained by proper social relationship.

Buddhism:

All existence is evil and results in miseries. Selfishness and desire are the roots of misery and suffering. Salvation is through suppressing desires, inner purity, and the necessity of re-incarnation.

Christianity:

God created man upright, but man fell into sin. "Wherefore, as one man sinned, sin entered into the world, and death by sin, and so death passed upon all men, for that all have sinned." "Out of his heart proceed all evils." Salvation is not a self-wrought thing, but it is a divine redemptive plan through the atonement of Jesus Christ by the regenerating agency of the Holy Spirit in saving and cleansing power. "Ye are saved by grace through faith."

CHAPTER II.

CHRIST AND MY HOME

THE PHYSICAL ENVIRONMENT

I was born in a heathen family in Foochow, South China. Later we moved our home into a little village about sixteen miles from the city.

Iang-kan, a typical, medieval, Chinese village where our old home was located, is situated at the base of a moderately high hill where southern fruits grow and where peculiar Chinese tea-flowers, "Mie-lee," scent the entire atmosphere in the summer. Its population is approximately eight hundred. There is only one main street through the village; the houses are uniformly built side by side only on one side facing the hill.

In front of the village there are several immense fish ponds, beside the street, in which the villagers raise fish and keep the waters for emergency purposes. Surrounding the village there are vast farms where the farmers raise their crops, three main harvests a year. The village is rather torn and old, yet its surroundings are the most picturesque and are a distinct type of Chinese medieval civilization.

There are three temples and one Ancestral Hall common to all in the village. The villagers are very religious, and they are strongly bound together in a common interest in their religious activities.

Our home is situated on the east side of the village. It is an old-fashioned building, yet it is of typical Oriental architecture of the medieval style. In front of the building there are high and wide stone steps which are raised above the general level of the street and lead up to the entrance of the gateway. The gateway leads to an open courtyard paved with big cut stones. Here we children congregated together and played inside the walls. From the courtyard there are still five more stone steps—academic steps—which lead to the Reception Hall. In the rear hall we shrined our ancestor's records and images. On both sides of the Hall are apartments for living rooms and bed rooms. Behind the Reception Hall there is another smaller hall—the Rear Hall—which we sometimes use for a dining-hall. Next to the Rear Hall is another smaller, open courtyard on both sides where our kitchens are located.

The whole enclosure is in the form of a parallelogram and surrounded by a high wall. It is a long and deep building divided into apartments. It is just a simple Chinese, big, tall, and one-story house, nothing like the five or six story houses the Europeans build, or the thirty or forty stories in the American skyscrapers. It is said that when a Chinese builds a house it occupies the land, but when an American builds a house it occupies the air. Chinese people sometimes inquire if it is the smallness of the territory that compels Western inhabitants to build their dwellings so near the clouds.

This village seems peaceful and cultural; all seem happy and contented, at least from a worldly standpoint, but nothing at all of a Christian religion is encouraged in the village.

THE RELIGIOUS ENVIRONMENT

Our home belonged to the three religions—Confucianism, Buddhism, and Taoism. My father was partly skeptic and Taoist; my mother was purely Taoist and Buddhist; sister and I were mixed in our religions, but I was especially a Confucianist. I accepted Confucianism as an ethical code of conduct and legalistic philosophy of moral life. Confucius to me was then "a perfect and complete Sage and holy Teacher of the ages." You may be wondering how we could get on together with these different faiths in this little home. Had these faiths not compromised with each other our home, I know, would have been in a terrible condition, at least as far as papa and mamma were concerned.

Mother sent me under private tutorship to study Confucius' Classics, Confucius' analects, etc.—the Chinese Bibles—when I was six years of age, and she dedicated me to a number of gods and goddesses, particudarly to one god to be his adopted son. I promised to bear his name and sign wherever I went until the age of sixteen if he would protect me from the evil spirits. I had to carry his name in a little yellow cloth-made sack hanging on my chest, sometimes outside and sometimes inside my coat, for we believed that if some evil spirits were to come to bother a child the god or goddess would come and rescue and fight against them.

Thus I belonged to these two families —human and spirit, visisible and invisible. We had to go to the Buddhist and Taoist temples, the general assembly, to worship twice a year with our offerings.   My mother fasted twice a month according to the Buddhist teaching under her religious conviction and obligation.   Chinese thus put themselves and their children in bondage and slavery to their idols through vows or through promises.   Big sums of money are being spent every year for idol-worship.   We were once living in darkness and superstition, but nobody told us a better way. We did our best according to our knowledge of religion and the sense of our reilgious duty.   We were honestly seeking for a true God who would save us from the sense of guilt and the unsafety of life, but pity to say, we took a wrong direction and knew not the right way. I say that the heathen cannot be condemned, but those who know the Way and have the Light, but hide it, shall be condemned.

Father died when I was less than one month old.   I never knew him except through the few things mother told me about him.   I do not understand what a father means to a child, for I have never had a father to bless my life, but I thank God for a good and noble mother to bless me.

Moreover, the fact about Christianity that means most to me is the Fatherhood of God with whom I have something to do. Taoism speaks of the horror of evil spirits; Buddhism preaches the solemnity and reverence of gods and goddesses; Confucianism teaches the dignity of a superior man; but Christianity talks about love and the Fatherhood of God! Here Christianity comes to the highest virtue when it says "Our Father who art in heaven. . . . ." I therefore believe that Christianity should prevail because it meets the human need.

Mother's heart was broken, and she suffered tremendously from the loss of her husband. The sorrow was unbearable. It was too heavy a stroke for this young widow with two children. We often saw her eyes wet during the lonely hours and weary nights. When I saw her tears my heart went out to her, and I wished that I could share her sorrow. Life became meaningless to her. She could find no joy and happiness on this earth. Life was to her but sorrow and suffering, and disappointment without escape. The world was just a solid mass against her, a mystery that could never be solved. She lost entirely her interest in life, confidence in men, and in religions which could give her but death, tears, misery, and trouble.

She was also greatly distressed over household matters and living, but she took courage and devoted herself to her children, and soon she started a tea business to support her family. Sister was a grown up girl and left home early to work and was soon married to a wealthy business man in the city.

Mother was often burdened and felt a great responsibility for me, the baby child, as to how to make me happy and to secure an adequate education for me. She committed me to the care of the gods. She went to the temple and prayed and worshipped seeking for something. Something? Yes, something that could uplift her soul, and something that could satisfy her heart's longing! Alas, she felt that her heart was just as heavy as usual! She went from one religion to another, but her life became more miserable. It was only more gods and more idolatries.

Living in this grim darkness and superstition the Devil blinded our eyes; the pain and misery we suffered were beyond description. Our hearts cried for the "Unknown God," and we looked for a way of deliverance. O, who can deliver us from the bondage of the sin and set us free? Who would break the chain of darkness and gladden our hearts that we might face life with hope and a smile? Only Christ!

From the soul there is a cry. From whence comes the rescue? God knows it and He hears it! From eternity God had a definite plan for this village and for this little Chinese family. God has prepared things for those who love Him that their ears never heard of and their eyes never saw. He can afford to wait long for the development of His redemptive plans and purposes. One day with Him is as a thousand years, and a thousand years as one day. But with finite man, whose term of life is measured by "three score years and ten" it is not so. Into this small village the dawn of Christianity began to break, and the mother of this little Chinese family was the first to see the light.

Confucianism:

"Recompense injury with justice, and recompense kindness with kindness." (Analects of Confucius 14:36).

Taoism:

"Recompense injury with kindness." (TTK 63:2). "To those who are good to me, I am good. And thus all to be good. To those who are sincere with me, I am sincere. And to those who are not sincere with me I am also sincere. And thus all get to be sincere." (TTK 49:2).

Christianity:

"But I say unto you which hear, Love your enemies, do good to them which hate you. Bless them that curse you, and pray for them that despitefully use you."
"But love ye your enemies, and do good, and lend, hoping for nothing again; and your reward shall be great, and ye shall be the children of the Highest; for he is kind unto the unthankful and to the evil." (Luke 6:27, 28, 35).

Confucius:

> The Way (Path) of Earth: "What you don't like to have done to yourself do not do unto others."   (D.O.M. 13:3).

Taoist:

> The Way of Heaven is to bless the good and make the bad miserable.   (S.B.E. 3:30).

Christ:

> The Way of Golden Mean: "Love your neighbor as yourself."

CHAPTER III.
CHRIST AND MY MOTHER

A GOSPEL MISSION

In 1916 a missionary and a Chinese preacher visited our village. They soon started a mission work in a demon-possessed house which the villagers would not use. The missionary repaired it for a Gospel Hall. The Chinese preacher's family was soon moved in and appointed to stay and work.

THE PERSECUTION

The villagers were, at first, very much interested in the newcomers and liked to talk to each other about the new doctrine—the Christianity— they brought in. The preacher tried hard to make an acquaintance with the people and to win them to Christianity. The result was very insignificant. The villagers did not care for the foreign religion. Soon a persecution arose in the village against the Christians.

"Down with the foreign religious invasion!" My mother found herself a leading figure among the women, as she was quite popular in the community. She possessed a fine, noble, and genial nature which caused her to be admired by all who knew her.

The people hated foreigners and missionaries alike because of the impression left by the British Opium War. They thought the foreigners came to our country with a religious mask to deceive our people and do harm to our nation. The Chinese Christians were, therefore, called "Traitors," "Foreigner's Dogs." The missionaries were called "Foreign Devils."

Our home was near to the Mission, but mother never attended it. She thought that all religions were universally the same. She did not like to take any more trouble to believe in the foreign doctrine, as she called it in that day. The preacher and the missionary tried hard to win her confidence and to talk to her about Christ. All effort seemed in vain. The missionary took a special interest in her and prayed for her. Did that prayer work? Yes, it did! The Lord answered a believing prayer in a most marvelous way.

MOTHER'S DREAMS

Early one morning a heavy conviction and fear came overwhelmingly upon her from a dream which occurred in three consecutive nights. In her dream she saw heaven open and a glorious mansion within. She found herself outside the heaven and rejected. She could not get in, but she could listen to the music which kept ringing in her ears even during the daytime. She was frightened and perplexed over this matter, since she found that she had no part in that beautiful land. She began to think about her sin and eternity and salvation. The more she thought the more miserable she became. The thought came that these Christian people might be right. From this time on she longed to be with the Christian people.

HER CONTACT WITH CHRISTIANS AND MISSIONARIES

The fourth day after this incident she went to the Mission to find the preacher. (The preacher did not go to find her; she went to find the preacher under the mighty influence of the Holy Spirit).

It was the first time that she had ever put her feet on any Christian ground, and it was her first contact with the Christians. She told the preacher about her dream and her conviction, asking permission if she might be able to see the missionary lady and visit her lodging place in which she expected that she might be able to see something like that which she had seen in the dream.

She was soon introduced to the missionary and was kindly invited to stay. She took me with her and planned to stay only two days. It was a day's journey. The new environment was quite different to us from what we usually had. Oh, we came to a Christian home. What a relief it brought to us. It was too good to leave the missionary home so soon. We were fortunately invited to stay for two weeks longer. Mother was intensely interested in the gospel the missionary presented to her. She was so eager to learn more about the truth and more and more about Jesus! Day and night she held the New Testament in her hands while she read it and re-read it and dwelled upon it. God gave mother a wonderful opportunity to hear the gospel and to learn about the truth which not only meant to her salvation, but also prepared her for the stand she had to take when she returned.

THE CONVERSION OF MOTHER

She was thoroughly converted in the missionary home through this visit.

When she came home she became a very earnest and firm Christian. The first thing she did when she came back was to burn down all the idols she had and to clean the house so that her family would be a family of God, and to start a family altar.

She stood up and gave her first testimony in public before hundreds of the villagers, witnessing to her new found faith and the joy she received therefrom. The changed life was so conspicuous and different from what she used to be. The news of her conversion was soon spread all over the villages round about. The people were greatly amazed at the new event of being a Christian in that day, as she was the first one to be a Christian in the village.

Soon a persecution raged all over the village as she would not take a part in idol worship nor give a penny for the purpose. A committee met considering what to do with her. The threatening words were given to her that Christians, who would not take part in any religious ceremonies, would not be allowed to stay in that community. She persisted in her faith unmovable, and remained loyal to Christ enduring the hardships, and willingly suffered material losses from the things which we used to enjoy from our Ancestral Hall.

A DEEPER EXPERIENCE THROUGH SUFFERING

She had once tried to persecute Christians, but now she was persecuted. She took her stand for Christ. She made up her mind that she would rather die than displease God and dishonor Jesus Christ. God blessed my mother and filled her with the Holy Spirit as a shining light among the heathen. She was very happy, bubbling up with joy. Her radiant and smiling face testified to what she possesed within!

Our home became a little heaven. We were so happy that we did not know what to do. I was quite small and could not understand her experience, but I knew some strange change had come to her which made it so real and happy. I understood that the gospel worked through the transforming power of the Holy Spirit. I saw the Gospel, God's redemptive power, which was so manifest in my mother's life before I was big enough to hear it and able to understand it. I thank God that the Gospel is not a mere theory, but the power of God unto salvation to every one that believes. It does work!

It is a touchstone, which, when it strikes the human heart, produces sparks and joys. This is the real conversion that will make people happy and radiant. It is the starting of a new life and a new adventure with God. It takes courage to be a Christian. To be a Christian means self-denial. To be a Christian in a non-Christian country means persecution, loss; and sometimes it means the danger of life. We will either stand or fall. A true religion will stand the test. Can you stand the test?

CALL TO THE MINISTRY

One year after her conversion the preacher left our village because the villagers rejected the Gospel. There was no church. Mother was the only Christian in the village. We were as an outcast family for Christ's sake. She was always loyal to Christ, rejoicing in the Lord.

On Sunday she kept the Lord's day and had family worship; sometimes we invited our neighbors to join in if they cared to. Sometimes we walked miles to a place where we hired a boat and crossed a river to a place where we could find a place to worship. It took a whole day's journey, both on land and on water, going and coming back from worship.

Mother had been a whole-hearted idol-worshipper, but now she was a strongly out-and-out Christian. A few years later she felt definitely called of

God to be His living witness. Without hesitating she gave up her prosperous business and consecrated herself wholly to the ministry. She now goes from one place to another to preach the Gospel which she once hated but which now she defends. I was one of the fruits of her ministry. She is still working for the Lord in China. Please pray for her.

There would be a volume to tell if I were to try to give her life in detail.

I do praise the Lord that Jesus Christ set us free from the bondage of sin and superstition and satisfies all of us today! In Him and Him alone we find peace, joy, hope, and life everlasting.

Friends, what Christ could do for my mother He can do for millions of mothers in China and also in America. I am burdened with the souls of mothers in China and mothers in other countries.

Of four hundred and fifty million Chinese people less than half of the population is comprised of women. Only one-fourth of the women have heard the

Gospel of Jesus Christ. The hope of China in the future rests with these Chinese mothers whose influence will denote what course the country will take. There is a tremendous responsibility as well as a challenge to the ministry of women in China today.

"Mary, when that little child
  Lay upon your heart at rest,
Did the thorns, Maid-mother, mild,
  Pierce your breast?

"Mary, when that little child
  Softly kissed your cheek benign,
Did you know, O Mary mild,
  Judas' sign?

"Mary, when that little child
  Cooed and prattled at your knee,
Did you see with heart beat wild,
  Calvary?"

—Rose Trumbull.

Confucius:

> "Filial piety is the root of all virtue, and the stem out of which grows all moral teaching. Our bodies, to every hair and bit of skin, are received by us from our parents; and we must not presume to injure or wound them." (S.B. E. 3:466).
>
> "The service of love and reverence to parents when alive, and those of grief and sorrow to them when they are dead: these completely discharge the fundamental duty of living men." (S.B.E. 3:488).

New Testament:

> "Children, obey your parents in the Lord: for this is right. Honor your father and mother; which is the first commandment with promise; that it may be well with thee, and thou mayest live long on the earth." (Eph. 6:1-3).
>
> "Your body is the temple of the Holy Ghost . . . . therefore glorify God in your body." (1 Cor. 6:15, 19, 20).

Christ:

> "He that loveth father or mother more than me is not worthy of me. . . ." (Matt. 10:37).
>
> "And every one that hath forsaken houses, or brethren, or sisters, or father, or mother, or wife, or children, or lands, for my name's sake, shall receive an hundredfold and shall inherit everlasting life." (Matt. 19:29).

The Mother and Son in the bond of ministry

Chapter IV.
CHRIST AND I

MOTHER'S INFLUENCE

As a result of mother's faith I was led to Christ and to the knowledge of the true and living God. Her beautiful Christian character and noble life and faith reflected on my soul and left an unperishing impression in my memory. I thank God a thousand times for such a wonderful and godly mother as she is to me. I owe to her not only material things but also spiritual help that I can never repay. God bless my dear mother!

When mother became a Christian I was rather small. She told me many of the Bible stories at night. I never had the privilege of attending Sunday school during my childhood, but I had this kind of Sunday school every night on my mother's lap and beside her bed.

SOME OF MY CHILDHOOD LIFE.

The Bible stories were much different

from the heathen stories which I heard. They were so strange and peculiar to me, and yet they were thrilling to my ears, stories such as Noah and the ark, Moses and the Exodus, and the Egyptians drowning in the Red Sea. The Bible was a mystery and a puzzle to me for awhile. However, the words of God were deeply down in the good soil of my heart until God gave it increase.

Once upon a time mother was reading the New Testament and came to Matthew 11:28-30, "Come unto me all ye that labor and are heavy laden, and I will give you rest . . . For my yoke is easy and my burden is light." She tried to commit these words to memory. She read them aloud and repeated them numbers of times. I was soon impressed by them and could memorize them right away—quicker than she did—yet without understanding their meaning. The content of this passage was quite strange to me. Why was His burden light, and how could a man heavy laden

get rest so easily?   Did it really mean
that when a coolie with a heavy burden
came to Jesus he would get rest and
would work no more?   Its actual meaning was misunderstood.   One day when
I came back from school I was called
from play by mother to carry some water for her to the kitchen. At first I was
not willing to do that, but since it was
mother's   command   I   involuntarily
obeyed.

When two buckets of water were
drawn from the well, I tried them and
found them quite heavy. "It was a hard
job."   Then Matthew 11:28-30 suddenly came to my mind like a flash.   Now
I said to myself that it was my time to
come to Jesus to get my burden lifted
and to find rest.   Then I knelt down on
my knees as mother used to do and offered my childish prayer.   It ran somewhat like this: "O, Jesus of my mother,
now I am coming to Thee as a laborer
with a heavy burden.   Give me rest, I
pray Thee, and make my loads lighter

so that I can carry them back to my mother, for Thy yoke is easy and Thy burden is light."

After I had prayed I quickly felt the load; it was just as heavy as before! The water and the buckets did not change in quality or in quantity. They remained just the same! I made another prayer, and another! The more I prayed the heavier the loads became.

I was greatly disappointed and began to doubt God's words because He failed to fulfil the promise to me. When I came home I was furious in temper, spilling water on the floor. It was not only because mother called me away from my play to carry the water, but also because the Bible meant nothing to me.

I could not understand these Scriptures until a few years later when I gave my heart to Jesus as my personal Savior. My sins were forgiven and my burden rolled away! What a glorious time that was!

"Rolled away! Rolled away!
　My burden of sin that was heavy,
　Has gone forever to stay.

"Rolled away! Rolled away!
　Oh, the joy that I felt
　At the cross as I knelt,
　My burden rolled away!"

He opened my eyes and gave me an understanding of His Word, showing me that it means when a sin-ladened soul comes to Jesus he will find rest and peace in his soul. You see the understanding comes after believing!

AN UP AND DOWN LIFE

I led an up and down life for some time. After having graduated from the government school I was induced to enter a Christian school, and later I became a preacher of the Cross instead of going to the navy and becoming an officer of authority.

Now, when I came to the Christian school, I had more contact with Christianity and learned more about the Bible, but I was then only a professing

Christian by name. Being brought up in a Christian home I took it for granted that mother was a Christian and I was naturally included, and everything would be, of course, all right. I read the Bible and went to church with mother. But these practices did not mean anything to me. I was not saved or born again. That was the trouble!

I did not know what it means to be a Christian. To become a Christian means to be converted, to be born again, and to be a follower of Christ. Is it not a pity to think that many of our so-called Christians today in our Christian countries are taking things for granted and facing spiritual things lightly? There has been too much of the mere horizontal and ceremonial Christianity, too much of using the rite of baptism for legal and communial purposes. Many people are doomed to hell before they realize it. God pity the merely professing Christians.

A careless and indifferent boy I

was thinking nothing about salvation, but all about self. Being satisfied in thought that I was a pretty good moral boy—perhaps the best in school—I was proud enough to think if all the students had my moral qualities the world would be different from what it is now. I planned after graduation to change the old country. Ambition? Oh, yes, it was great ambition! Young people are dreamers. Human nature is the same over the world. Alas, what a sin of pride it is. I could not see my sinful condition and the need of salvation.

Well, sometimes I was somewhat led to think about my soul and about eternity. I was anxious then to be saved. I was in agony many times about my wrong doings and desired to be delivered, but no one could show me the way of deliverance, because they thought I was a Christian. No one knew or understood my condition and the struggle going on in my heart but God. I heard much about the free gift of salvation, but I could not see it that all came by grace. The salvation seemed to be too cheap and too easy.

MY CONVERSION AND DEEPER EXPERIENCE

In 1927 God gave me a quiet time; I was led to read the Bible honestly, thoughtfully, and prayerfully. The Holy Spirit opened my eyes, and the Lord graciously revealed Himself to me by His words which made the way of salvation so clear and plain.

I began to see myself in the light of His words, that I was a lost sinner even though I was reared in a Christian home by a saintly mother. Mother's religion was good, but it could not satisfy me. She could not take salvation for me. Everybody must take a stand before the judgment seat of God. Everyone must take and drink the Water of Life by himself in order to be saved. Salvation cannot be inherited through blood. I saw it now!

God's words pierced through all my

secret thoughts, and I found myself as stated in Isaiah 64:6, "We are all as an unclean thing, and all our righteousnesses are as filthy rags." I acknowledged my sins before him and cried out for salvation. Praise God, He not only showed me the sins, but also showed me a way out. There came the vision of the crucified One nailed on the cross for my sins. Jesus, the Son of God, took away the penalty of the sins, and my sins were nailed on the cross. Yes, Jesus the Savior was what I wanted.

There in my room alone with God, with open Bible, and with an open heart I accepted Jesus Christ as my personal Savior. He was no longer a guest in my home, nor my mother's God, nor a historical One, but my Savior, King and All!

> "Could my tears forever flow,
> Could my zeal no languor know,
> These for sin could not atone;
> In my hands no price I bring;
> Simply to thy cross I cling."

Oh, friends, it was a real experience,

and it was a new life beginning with God. Thank God that I am a sinner saved by grace. The sense of guilt was removed; sin was forgiven by the power of the Blood of Jesus Christ. "I know whom I have believed and am persuaded that He is able to keep that which I have committed unto Him against that day."

I was brought to a glorious experience in Christ, not through any enticing words of a preacher, nor through the preaching of a missionary, but only through the reading of God's Word. Now the Bible became a very interesting and new Book to me; I desired to read it more. The more I read, the more I saw the truth. I believed that the Bible was inspired by the Holy Ghost. It is the infallible words of God; it contains truth only, and nothing but the truth from first to last. I put my heart, and sometimes my tears on the Bible. Praise the Lord that I was saved, sanctified, and kept on being satisfied!

MY ASSURANCE OF SALVATION

For sometime I was troubled with a problem that caused me to doubt and wonder how I could know that I was saved. Suppose I should die tonight; how would I know that I would go to heaven and not to hell; and what was the basis of my belief for my eternal security?

This became the great problem that often robbed away my joy and peace, that brought me to a state of perplexity and uncertainty. I did not enjoy my religion as much as I should.

I heard many church people say that nobody could know that he was saved until after his death and coming to the Judgment Seat when God would bring forth the verdict. I asked several church people if they knew that they were saved or born again. Many were not able and dared not to answer me. Some were bold enough to say that they were, perhaps, saved, or, maybe, were saved, and the like; some took the attitude that they hoped to be saved on the account of going to church and reading the Bible.

I could see that there might be some wrong in their faiths, but I found myself in the same position of uncertainty and doubts. I soon realized that unless I could positively know that I was saved, or had some assurance about my salvation I would be just as superstitious as any heathen. If Christianity could not assure my personal salvation Christianity was not the best religion. I had better give up my faith.

I took up a scientific and earnest attitude to study the Bible and to seek the truth. "Seek and ye shall find." I believed that the good Lord would never fail those who sought after Him.

"Blessed are they who do hunger and thirst after righteousness, for they shall be filled."

I believe only God's Word will solve all the problems, and His Word alone is the solid rock upon which I will build my faith. A true faith cannot build on air; it must rest on or hold to the unchangeable Word of God.

For several consecutive days of careful and prayerful study of the Bible with the guidance of the Holy Spirit and the Christian friends' help I discovered the following truth:

I. The Way of Salvation.

1. Repentance.—"Repent ye therefore, and be converted, that your sins may be blotted out." (Acts 3:19; 17:30).

2. Faith—"Believe on the Lord Jesus Christ, and thou shalt be saved, and thy house." (Acts 16:30, 31).

3. Confession.—"And with the mouth confession is made unto salvation." (Rom. 10:9, 10).

I thank God I met the above conditions. Didn't you?

II. The Knoweldge of Salvation.

The salvation is the knowable thing. 1 John 5:13 says, "These things have I written unto you that believe on the name of the Son of God; that ye *may* know that ye have eternal life." This Scripture challenged my faith. I may and can know if I have eternal life. Then St. John 5:24—"Verily, verily I say unto you, he that heareth my word, and believeth on him that sent me, hath everlasting life, and shall not come into condemnation; but is passed from death unto life," gripped my soul. It stands in my memory as bright as the noonday. I believe I will remember it throughout eternity! I found five truths in this verse, as follows:

1. "He that heareth my word"—I did. "How shall they believe in him of whom they have not heard?" (Rom. 10:14).

2. "and believe on him"—Yes, I also did! "So then faith cometh by hearing, and hearing by the word of God." (Rom. 10:17).

3. "hath everlasting life"—This phrase struck me hard and it woke me up to the fact that I have already the

eternal life and that I am already saved, because God says so; therefore, I know it is so. I do not need to wait for or to hope to, because I have already possessed it. God has spoken it; it is enough!

4. "and shall not come into condemnation"—Praise the Lord for the Scripture also says, "there is, therefore, now no condemnation to them which are in Christ Jesus." (Rom. 8:1). The blood of Jesus cleansed me from all sin, it purged my conscience from the dead work to serve the living God without fear; whereby we cry Abba Father. (Rom. 8:18; Heb. 9:14; 1 John 1:9).

5. "but is passed from death unto life."—I do not need to wait until after the death. It is passed. It is clear, and it is settled forever! With this basis of assurance I am ready to face God with joy.

III. The Enjoyment of the Salvation.

The "Sprinkled Blood" makes me safe; the "Spoken Word" makes me sure; and the "Assurance of Salvation" causes me to be happy and to enjoy my religion.

The elder son of the Israelite is happy because he knows the sprinkled blood is applied on the door. He is safe because the Lord has spoken it.

"Therefore, with joy shall ye draw water of the wells of salvation" (Isa. 12:3). It is the "joy of salvation."

IV. The Security of the Salvation.

"He is able to save them to the uttermost that come unto God by him, seeing he ever liveth to make intercession for them."

Our safety hangs on Christ's work *for* us; our assurance hangs on God's Words *to* us; and our enjoyment or joy depends on a knowledge of our salvation and not grieving the Holy Spirit *in* us.

The danger for average Christians mixing up with the enjoyment and security. There are vast differences between these two things. We may lose our joy and peace and the fellowship or communion with God because of sin, but it does not mean that we lose our salvation again which is in Jesus Christ, our Savior and Lord. The Scripture says that "Whosoever believeth in him should not perish." (John 3:16). "And I give unto them eternal life; and they shall never perish, neither shall any man pluck them out of the Father's hand." (John 10:28).

Joy, peace, or communion with God may be and will be restored through the confession of sin. "We have fellowship one with another, and the blood of Jesus Christ his Son cleanseth us from all sin." (1 John 1:7).

With this assurance of my faith in and knowledge of Him I will shout with St. Paul through eternity,—"Who shall separate me from the love of Christ? Shall tribulation, or distress, or persecution, or famine, or nakedness, or peril, or sword? Nay, in all these things we are more than conquerors through him that loved us. For I am persuaded, that neither death, nor life, nor angels, nor principalities, nor powers, nor things present, nor things to come, nor height, nor depth, nor any other creature, shall be able to separate us from the love of God, which is in Jesus our Lord."

MY CALL TO THE MINISTRY

One year later, in 1928, I faced the great problem of my life plan. A strong conviction pointing toward the ministry and many other worldly plans confronted me. I was at a great loss as to which way I should turn. It was as if I was brought up to a high mountain and showed all the glories of the plain. The devil whispered to me and said, "All these things will I give thee, if thou wilt fall down and worship me."

I did not want to be a preacher because that meant too much sacrifice. I wanted to be an easy Christian. I reasoned with myself that it would be just as well to be a business man earning money and supporting some missionaries or preachers as to devote my whole time to the ministry. I then prayed to God to bless my way. I keenly felt that there might be something wrong in my prayer and in my devotion. I sent for mother to come and pray with me and for me.

I told mother about my conviction, my struggles, and my plans. We prayed and wept, but no answer came because my-Self was too strong. I had too many plans which shut out the "Small Voice."

For several days I went through a great many major battles fighting for a way out—Mammon or God? Money or Gospel? Ministry or Business? Crown or Cross?

I was very uneasy about myself, without peace and joy. Pacing back and forth in my room, contemplating on this life matter, I knew I had to make a decision for God or the devil. Should

I say to God yes or no?   Here was the test of my faith, a life crisis depended on what I chose.

I went to prayer but found nothing to say.   God whispered to me, "Won't you surrender all to me, or have me not at all?"   I thought it over, and I soon burst out with crying as I considered the Suffering One.   His love constrained me.   I was conquered! My lips moved, and my heart melted.   Then I said, "Yes, Lord, I now surrender all to thee.   I am Thine and Thou art mine."

MY CONSECRATION

There on my knees I consecrated myself to God for His service and pledged myself to Him to preach the Gospel throughout the Empire of China.

This consecration meant giving up my study to be a business man and many other fond ambitions.   It might also mean persecution, cross-bearing, and being despised by friends and relatives.   I gladly assented and answered His call.   I put all my future in His hands.   If He called me He would take care of me financially and intellectually.   There was no longer a struggle.   I arose from my knees with a sense of inward refining and calmness and of the fullness of the abundant life that I had never known before.   The deeper adjustment to Christ's mind and purpose, and God's best plan for my life had been brought by a deeper surrender.

As soon as I got up from my knees I wrote in my diary about this consecration service and the crucifixion of self, "I am crucified with Christ, and no longer I, but Christ lives in me."   It was the first day of January, 1928, when this experience took place at Pagoda Anchorage, Foochow, South China.   Praise the Lord!

MY YOUNG MINISTRY

I started out in my ministry as a young preacher at the age of eighteen. I could not preach at first, but I could testify wherever I went. I did personal work in churches, schools, stores, hospitals, prisons, on the road and on the boat. I had found a way of life which fully and entirely satisfied, and I did not care to keep it all to myself. I wanted to make it known that others might share with me this blessed experience in the saving knowledge of Jesus Christ.

If you are really born again and start a new life, it means work, service and growth. You cannot keep from telling others of that which you have found and now enjoy.

A Christian experience is precious, and it is the highest privilege and pleasure that any human being can have in experiencing the blessed and heavenly fellowship with God. We simply cannot afford to keep it for our own. Something we possess within will express itself without. This is the normal Christian attitude toward life.

I do praise the Lord that He has

chosen me, the unworthy one, to proclaim this glorious Gospel and use me as the means of bringing others into the way of truth. I also praise the Lord that in the past seven years He has been leading me to do evangelistic work in China, meeting and preaching to all classes of people—to Confucianists, Buddhists, Taoists, to the low and high, to the rich and poor, to the educated and illiterate, to the young and old, both in private and public, in schools, in hospitals, and in jails, and any place in which I could find an opportunity to win some for Jesus. I especially thank God for the privileges given to me in the past two years in traveling in several foreign countries, both in the United States of America and in Europe, testifying to all people concerning the saving power of Jesus Christ to all people alike, regardless of race, nationality, color, or creed!

THE GOSPEL

Our Gospel is big enough for all people. It is a free salvation for all men. The blood of Jesus can cleanse us from all sin. "I am not ashamed of the gospel of Christ, for it is the power of God unto salvation to every one that believeth."

I have no apology for preaching the Gospel, for it is God's message to all lost humanity. We are to preach Christ, not only as a Teacher, but as a Savior. It is this which gives us a complete and sufficient message for the requirements of all men.

This is not a man-made Gospel. It is God's own Word concerning His redemptive plan for a lost world. It is God's great and gracious gift for lifting the bonds of sin-burdened humanity. The Gospel then testifies to a conviction that God has spoken, that there is a message clothed with God's own certainty, adequate to meet man's tragic needs!

MY TEMPTATION

I was once offered an opportunity to go into a business that would lead me to wealth, but away from the track of preaching the Gospel. But what things were gain to me, those I counted loss for Christ. Christ has called me to preach the Gospel. Woe unto me if I preach not the Gospel. I would rather go with Christ in poverty than live in wealth and luxury without Him.

My brother-in-law is a wealthy business man in Foochow. He can get anything that can be puchased with money, but he is without Christ and an unhappy man. He thinks that I am a big fool wasting my time in a work that brings no increase in worldly goods. But I praise the Lord, for He has called me to a work that makes others rich in the faith and has eternal value and reward. There is a crown waiting for me if I am faithful unto death. "Lay not up thy treasure on earth, but lay up thy treasure in heaven." Thank God that Christ is everything to me today!

COMING TO AMERICA

I am young and I need more training. The Lord has wonderfully opened a way for me to come to America for further preparation and education that I may go back and be more efficient in His service. I came to America in 1933 and entered Asbury College which I have found to be the most adequate place for me and all Christian people wishing a college education. I thank God that Asbury College is such a unique institution with high Christian ideals and principles.

A great many good friends of mine kindly warned me that if I went to America I would lose my experience, for America and her materialism and modernism would spoil my faith. But I think that no place on earth is safe to one if he is out of God's will. I thank God for His keeping grace that has kept me until now safe and sound in His faith and truth. Moreover, I am growing in grace and in the knowledge of

Jesus Christ.　Jesus means more and more to me every day.　To any person who knows God deep enough Christ ought to mean more and more to him every day.

America is surely a great nation with all her materialism and wealth, but these do not make America great. It is the faith of the Pilgrim fathers! It is truly a sad thing to see the inscription on coins that "In God We Trust" while people and churches are far away from God.　In my opinion there is no Christian land on earth, but I do meet Christians in every nation.　I did not come to see Christian America, but I did expect to see some American Christians. I have met many of the best Christians in America, but, at the same time, I have seen the worst sinners in this country. America needs Christ! "Faith of our fathers! Holy faith!"

All need Christ.　The world is in a desperate dying condition without Christ.　Jesus Christ is the only solution for all the problems of the world today. The more I study the more I am convinced that Christ is the All-sufficient Savior who can meet all our needs individually and internationally.

BUDDHA AND CHRIST.

Buddha:

1. The Noble Truth of Suffering:
   Birth is suffering; death is suffering; presence of hatred is suffering; absence of love is suffering; to wish and not to get is suffering; briefly, the five-fold nature by which beings cling to existence is suffering.

2. The Noble Truth of Cause of Suffering:
   Desire is the cause; it leads from birth to birth, bringing with it delight and longing, seeking its gratification here and there—namely, desire for sensual pleasure, desire for existence, desire for prosperity.

3. The Noble Truth of the Cessation of Suffering:
   Suffering ceases with the cessation of this desire—a cessation consisting in the absence of every passion—with the abandoning of desire, with the doing away with it, with deliverance from it, with the destruction of it.

Christ:

The Divine Truth of Cause of Suffering:
In the world you shall have tribulation, suffering pain, grief, and sorrow. There shall be wars, rumors of war, famines, pestilences, earthquakes in divers places, and persecutions for religious causes. The whole creation groaneth and travaileth in pain together until now.

2. The Divine Truth of Case of Suffering:
   Suffering is because of sin; it is the result of one's wrong choice and evil social order or environment, and natural forces. "Cursed is the ground for thy sake; in sorrow shalt thou eat of it all the days of thy life." (Gen. 3:17).

3. The Christian Attitude Toward Suffering:
   In the world you shall have tribulation or suffering, but be of good cheer; I have overcome the world. We glory in tribulation knowing that tribulation worketh patience, and pa-

tience, experience, and experience, hope. The Christian takes the sufferings and admits them into the purpose of his life, making them contribute to higher ends, an d using them for the glory of God. "For our light affliction which is but for a moment, worketh for us a far more exceeding and eternal glory." The Christian uses suffering for good and is able to triumph over it. Through the suffering he looks to the future glory.

* * * *

If Jesus Christ is a man,
   And only a man, I say,
That of all mankind I cleave to him,
   And to him I will cleave alway.
If Jesus Christ is a God,
   And the only God, I swear,
I will follow him through heaven and hell,
   The earth, the sea, and the air.

                        —Sel.

CHAPTER V

CHRIST AND CHINA

THE HISTORIC NATION

China always appeals to me most because of her vastness, masses of people, riches of resources, and because of the beauty of the land, and the antiquity of her civilization

She is known as one of the oldest and largest nations in the world. Here in this country we can find the most ancient and medieval people, culture, and customs, and yet at the same time the most advanced type of life.

Our history goes back as far as any historian can trace the record of more than four thousand years. We have the record of Noah's flood and the derivation of our race. We speak the language and observe the same social and political customs and enjoy the great eastern civilization that we did years ago before the Christian era. We are

the only living representative today of
people and government which were con-
temporary with the Egyptians, the As-
syrians, and the Jews as a nation.

HEATHENISM AND CHINESE CIVILIZA-TION

China has, for centuries, devoted herself to the heathen religions. She became a land of idolatry and of many
gods. Chinese people are very religious; for centuries they have been seeking their happiness from the things that
are made of stones, woods, silver, and
gold. Chinese people are seemingly satisfied with their hand-made religions.

Confucianism, Taoism, and Buddhism are the national religions. Among
these Confucianism has made a great
contribution to the nation and to her
moral and intellectual life. Confucius
has made China great. He will play a
large part in the making of the China
that is to be.

Chinese civilization grew up from the

influence of the heathen religions which stimulated arts, literatures, and ethics, and placed the education and public ethical life on a foundation that upheld the nation until this present century.

The Empire has, furthermore, been upheld by the rigorous social obligation due to the superiors in family and state by the constant emphasis placed on Confucius' moral or ethical teaching and the constant worship on the part of the people of the departed spirits of their ancestors.

The Chinese are practical, and Confucius has ministered to that bent with such insight and wisdom that the whole life of the people has been built up around his ideals. The Chinese have deep spiritual longing and a capacity for mystical religion which many are not likely to appreciate. Taoism so soon descended to the level of quackery that all it could do was to trade on the superstitions and fear of the people. But still there was an unsearched depth to the Chinese heart which nothing in China had been able to touch. This was the opportunity in China for Buddhism.

COMING OF BUDDHISM

The Emperor Ming dreamed one night that a golden figure with two arrows in his hand was standing in his palace court. His soothsayers interpreted the dream to be the revelation that a great personality was born in the West to whom the Emperor must send an embassy. The embassy reached India in 64 A. D., and carried away with them Buddhist idols and books which were being interpreted into Chinese. These soon took on a Chinese aspect and style and have remained so ever since.

The old Emperor was seeking truth for himself and for his own people. Thus Buddhism entered China, making a great contribution by adding greater numbers of gods to that country.

Had the Chinese found what they wanted? Could Buddhism satisfy their national and individual lives? The presence of a million Buddhist monks and nuns today in China speak of the unfortunate life of these people. Life to them is a suffering, a curse, and a sorrow. There is no escape except the ending of all the desires which leads to the way of Nirvana. Their lives are not examples worthy of emulation, for they have brought discredit to the whole brotherhood.

We are assured that many of the monks, thousands of them, deplore the condition they are in. Here are souls seeking emancipation, who resist wrong doing and lewdness as they would a pestilence, and who are reaching out in every way they know to find the light. They have not really found it!

I am not condemning the religions. They all contain some very good ideals and some truth. They are not necessarily superstitious. In fact, I owe much to these faiths. I was born with a spirit of reverence and godliness that

I count valuable. I respected all religious convictions and spiritual things, seeking for truth and craving to walk in the way of golden mean. I owe much to the influence of these faiths, yet these faiths are utterly inadequate to minister to my inner and deepest need.

WHY I BECAME A CHRISTIAN

There are three steps which led me to Christianity, and there are four reasons why I became a Christian. They are as follows:

1. I was first convinced and believed that there is one true and eternal God in the universe, the Creator of all things and the absolute Cause of everything.

2. From the belief of the monotheistic God I quickly sensed a duty and obligation toward Him as a creature. I found myself "astrayed" apart from the Source of Life. "I am undone, and come short of his glory." A sense of guilt was created in me.

3. With a sense of guilt I sought for a way out and a way up, back to my Origin, with longing for a deliverance. In a state of bewilderment and hunger I wandered through the gate of Confucianism, and I entered into the hall of Taoism and Buddhism searching through every corner of the religions and at last came to a side door of Skepticism where I fortunately met Christianity who kindly introduced me to a Person who told me that "He is the Way, the Truth, and the Life: no man cometh unto the Father, but by Me." He is the Son of God, and came from God. He that is sent of God is able to bring me back to God. Then I told Him, "Lead on, and I will follow!"

My reasons for following Him are:

1. Christ, the Person, is divine. Buddha and Confucius and other leaders of religions were humans who died and were buried, but Christ rose from the dead and lives forever. He is able to save to the uttermost all who come

unto God by Him.   He is the Resurrection and the Life. He conquered sin and death and opened the gate of paradise into the life everlasting.   Christ is the center of Christianity.

2.   Christianity alone gives me an adequate, clear, and consistent view of God.   It presents Him as the one God, eternal, infinite, omnipotent, omniscient; perfect in wisdom, in righteousness and holiness; and yet merciful, gracious, full of goodness and love, a true Father in His feelings and acting toward men.   Christianity shows God as a Father in relation to men.

3.   Only Christianity brings men into a right relationship with God through the atonement of Jesus Christ.   It reveals to us a truth that men can find God.   In fact, God is finding men, and men have a possible way of access to God in complete communion and fellowship with Him. Only Christianity shows the perfect union of the divine and the human in the perfect life of Christ.

4. Only Christianity is the absolute religion that offers a satisfactory plan of salvation or deliverance from sins. Christ is the manifestation of God, and took the form of man—the Word made flesh. He bore the sin of the world on the cross, shedding His blood for the remission of sin. Through this vicarious suffering, Christ opened the way to the Sanctuary.

Christianity teaches not only about death, but also about life. Death deals with sin, but life is the Christian new adventure with God. So Christ must die and also rise up from the dead and live. He is the perfect Divine for the Savior of the world; He is the perfect Human for the Example of the believers.

Therefore, I believe that Christianity is the true and the absolute religion, the only true and intrinsically valid religion. It, to my conviction, must ultimately become the religion of China, my beloved native land, and of the whole world today!

COMING OF CHRISTIANITY

According to one of our old and vague Chinese traditions, we are told that one of Christ's disciples, Thomas, crossed the Indian Ocean and came to visit China. He also appeared to one of our kings in the palace court. We often wonder why our Emperor did not accept Christianity as he did Buddhism. Nobody knows.

Passing by this vague, yet thrilling, story it seems certain that Nestorian monks driven out of the Roman Empire penetrated into western China as early as 505 A. D. They were received with favor at Hsianfu in Shensi, where the court then was. Their churches flourished and multiplied for a time, but their religion was of a somewhat low type, showing an evident accommodation to Chinese beliefs. They gradually disappeared like a foam on the water, leaving nothing but a stone to tell of their existence and their churches dating from 781. It is a very famous stone, the oldest Christian monument in the Empire, and perhaps in all Asia, the birth-continent of our faith. It was discovered in 1625.

Rome's first missionary to the Chinese was John of Monte Corvino who arrived in 1293 via India. Later he was followed by Jesuits and many others. These early missionaries attempted to Christianize China, but their efforts are reckoned a complete failure.

The Roman Catholic missions have done more harm than good to China. Their work has been altogether too political, too despotic, too ceremonial, and too dogmatic. They lean too much on foreign civil government, trusting largely on diplomacy, intrigue, and the military power for the advancement of their interests. They interfere too much with the government of the country to which they go. This has been one of the chief troubles in China. From the beginning until now it has stirred up great hostility against Christianity,

Protestant missions included.

In 1807 the Protestant missions and faith came to China. Robert Morrison was the pioneer of the Protestants. A glimpse of Christian truth began to shine into that darkest land. China´s looking for the light, and she is ready!

A SPIRITUAL HUNGER AND EXPECTATION

The Chinese people have kept an oral tradition for generations. They were told to look for a "Coming One" or "The Son of Heaven." They studied stars and watched the water in the Yellow River. When the water in the Yellow River becomes clean and clear, and when the Star appears the Son of Heaven will come. Before my mother became a Christian she used to get up early and watch the morning stars with a hope of finding a Star of the Coming One. She often sighed and said, "Oh, how I wish that the Son of Heaven would come soon!" Long years rolled on before the weary soul was suddenly gladdened and strangely warmed when she found that One in Christianity.

The Jews looked for the Messiah; the Chinese looked for the Son of Heaven; the Wise Men from the East watched for the Bethlehem Star; the heathen people worshipped the "Unknown God;" and the civilized people are seeking for reality. Men are all religious, and are all interested in religions. On every hand men are looking for the One who can make the earth a fit place in which to live.

There is everywhere a spiritual expectancy. There are untold numbers of people who are hungry for spiritual things. The church and the Christians are facing an incomparable challenge. How helpless we are without the burning motive of Christ's love and endowment of power from above! The present hour brings the Christian church its greatest danger and at the same time its greatest challenge and opportunity.

THE NEW CHINA

Now the new generation has arisen, and China has awakened to her need. A great change has come upon the whole face of the nation. She is now facing the challenges from other countries.

Old faiths have been thrown overboard, and the new faith is discountenanced. Passions are aroused; ideals and principles are classified. In fact, there is progress and improvement in every line, yet nothing is offered which will really satisfy the spiritual yearning of the younger generation. The young people today are brought up without any religious faith whatsoever. They are rather careless and indifferent about religious matters and are drifting in the atheistic stream.

Today there are several dynamic forces—such as Nationalism, Communism, Militarism, Skepticism, and Christianity—at work fashioning a new China and threatening to shape her destiny for the future. The result of the clash of these forces which are now struggling for the soul of China is to leave things in a state of utter bewilderment. These, then, are the forces which are hastening China toward a decisive hour!

China's hope for tomorrow is in Christianity. China is facing a crisis as never before in her history.

COMMUNISM OR CHRIST

There are two great forces engaged in a life and death struggle for the soul of the great country—Materialism or Communism, and Christ.

I look to China with great hope for the future. She has undergone a tremendous change politically, educationally, and economically in recent years. She has been awakening to her needs as never before. Japanese invasion, on the other hand, in my opinion, has also done some good as an undisputed force to stimulate national integrity and to help to unify the country. A great renaissance is just ahead of her. My prediction is that her national and religious tendency will bend toward Christianity because Christianity only has something to offer to that nation, and only Christianity cares for their souls.

There is a strong Christian movement in China today which moves the nation. The young Christian people rise up and take the burdens on their shoulders, carrying the Gospel to their own people with a pure motive and bare hands, living by faith and depending on God's promises. Such a presentation of undying love, unselfishness, and sacrificial Christ-like spirit we have scarcely ever seen in the Christian history of China. A strong national spiritual awakening and a nation-wide revival are on the way!

Some people say that Communism is very strong in China, but I say that Christianity is stronger than any other force in China today.

Christianity has unfortunately been misinterpreted and colored by some missionaries with their western civilization and their native ways. They have forced the Chinese Christians to follow and imitate them. Thus Christianity has been taken as a white-man's religion with the Chinese feeling themselves utter strangers to it. They want to have nothing to do with it. The Anti-Christian movement was only an inevitable and spontaneous reaction.

Now Christianity is being rightly interpreted by the natives with their native genius and life. Chinese people accept the eastern Christianity and feel better adjusted to the Person, Christ, as the Bible purely sets Him forth.

THE MOST URGENT NEED

The most urgent need at the present time is already demonstrated in the fact that Christ can and does satisfy the soul of China and has perfectly satisfied me and a great multitude. Yet there is a still great number who have not had their first opportunity to hear the Gospel of Jesus Christ, and there are many places where Christ has never yet been named.

For years missionaries and Chinese preachers have made a great sacrifice trying to go into the interiors to evangelize, yet most of the work is being done in the big towns and port cities. I am burdened with the souls of China's millions, both for her spiritual and physical welfare. There are thousands of young people with much more ability than I have, but they have never had the opportunity of hearing the Gospel of Jesus Christ, and some of them have never had an opportunity of learning. My heart is burning with zeal for these precious souls of future young China.

There must be unselfish evangelistic campaigns which will require more sacrificial and self-denying service throughout the entire nation. In China we need a nation-wide evangelism, group evangelism, personal evangelism, camp evangelism, and town evangelism. To this end the church of China must possess a new life from Christ for herself and must have a systematic and true presentation of the Christian Gospel of Christ to the nation as a whole. It is not to be achieved by force, more organization, new creed, or material might. These are but outward expressions of the inner life. The important thing is to give China a Christ. Christ must not be interpreted as a Western God, nor as a purely Eastern figure, but as a Savior of the world and the Brother of all men and the Friend of sinners!

For this program we need born-again and sanctified native workers and God-called missionaries. It is not more missionaries, but missionaries who are called of God and filled with the Holy Spirit. They must preach the Word of Life, and know how to point men to Jesus.

I believe that there is no other nation which needs Christ more, nor does any country offer more opportunities for the spreading of the Gospel than China today. China needs Christ! Shall we win that nation for Christ? Shall we give God a chance? Please help us!

IF

If we could get a vision of a lost and dying world,
And realize that souls just now to hell are being
      hurled,
If we could get a vision of the awfulness of sin,
We'd linger not one moment, but seek some soul to
      win.
If we would spend a little while each day upon our
      knees,
We'd so enriched with blessings be our zeal would
      never freeze,
If we could get the vision of our possibility here
Burnt up would be our bridges; to God's will we'd
      steer.
If we could catch a vision of the scene on Calvary's
      brow,
Unfettered true devotion to Christ we all would vow.
If we could visualize Him rise triumphant over the
      tomb,
We'd never be downhearted or e'er give way to
      gloom!
If every Nazarene were filled with the Holy Ghost
No one would dream of going back, or dare to leave
      his post.
If we could get the vision our movement would ad-
      vance
God is able now to use us, He only waits a chance!
—Joe Irvine, Scotland.

THE MISSIONARY

O, matchless honor all unsought,
High privilege surpassing thought,
That Thou shouldst call me, Lord, to be
Linked in work-fellowship with Thee;
To carry out Thy wondrous plan,
To bear Thy messages to man;
Intrust with Christ's own word of grace
To every soul of human race.

—Sel.

www.ingramcontent.com/pod-product-compliance
Lightning Source LLC
Chambersburg PA
CBHW071916120726
48001CB00005B/1759